Half Hollow Hills

WITHDRAWN

Community Library

D1709790

Fact Finders®

ADVENTURES ON THE AMERICAN FRONTIER

STRANDED IN THE SIERRA NEVADA

THE STORY OF THE DONNER PARTY

BY DANIELLE SMITH-LLERA

Consultant:
Ethan Rarick
Author of *Desperate Passage: The Donner Party's Perilous Journey West*

HALF HOLLOW HILLS
COMMUNITY LIBRARY
55 Vanderbilt Parkway
Dix Hills, NY 11746

CAPSTONE PRESS
a capstone imprint

Fact Finders are published by Capstone Press,
1710 Roe Crest Drive, North Mankato, Minnesota 56003
www.capstonepub.com

Copyright © 2016 by Capstone Press, a Capstone imprint. All rights reserved. No part of this publication may be reproduced in whole or in part, or stored in a retrieval system, or transmitted in any form or by any means, electronic, mechanical, photocopying, recording, or otherwise, without written permission of the publisher.

LIBRARY OF CONGRESS CATALOGING-IN-PUBLICATION DATA
Smith-Llera, Danielle, 1971–
  Stranded in the Sierra Nevada: The Story of the Donner Party/by Danielle Smith-Llera.
    pages cm.—(Fact finders: Adventures on the American frontier)
  Summary: "Examines the expedition of the Donner Party by discussing how they came to be stranded in the Sierra Nevada Mountains and the immediate and lasting effects their journey had on the nation as well as the people and places involved"—Provided by publisher.
  Audience: Grades 4–6.
  Includes bibliographical references and index.
  ISBN 978-1-4914-4898-4 (library binding); ISBN 978-1-4914-4912-7 (paperback);
  ISBN 978-1-4914-4930-1 (ebook PDF)
  1. Donner Party—Juvenile literature. 2. Pioneers—California—History—19th century—Juvenile literature.
3. Pioneers—West (U.S.)—History—19th century—Juvenile literature. 4. Overland journeys to the Pacific—Juvenile literature. 5. Frontier and pioneer life—West (U.S.)—Juvenile literature. 6. Sierra Nevada (Calif. and Nev.)—History—19th century—Juvenile literature. I. Title.
  F868.N5S48 2015
  979.4'4--dc23   2015008296

EDITORIAL CREDITS
Jennifer Huston, editor; Kazuko Collins, designer;
Tracy Cummins, media researcher; Laura Manthe, production specialist

PHOTO CREDITS
Capstone Press: 11; Getty Images: Historic Map Works LLC, 21, New York Public Library, 24; Jim Carson: jimcarsonstudio.com, Cover, 5 (top), 18–19; North Wind Picture Archives: 6, 12; Courtesy Scotts Bluff National Monument: 8; Shutterstock: Itana, Design Element, ixer, Design Element, Picsfive, Design Element; Wikimedia: 5 (bottom), Bancroft Library, 23, 27, The Expedition of the Donner Party and Its Tragic Fate/Eliza P. Donner Houghton, 22, 26, Google Art Project, 17, NARA, 15.

PRIMARY SOURCE BIBLIOGRAPHY
Page 4, callout quote: Virginia Reed Murphy and Karen Zeinert, ed. *Across the Plains in the Donner Party.*
        North Haven, Conn.: Linnet Books, 1996, p. 14.
Page 9, Line 17, callout quote, and sidebar: Eliza Poor Donner Houghton. *The Expedition of the Donner Party and
        Its Tragic Fate.* Chicago: A.C. McClurg & Co., 1911, pp. 24, 25.
Page 13, callout quote: *Across the Plains in the Donner Party.* pp. 38, 41.
Page 16, callout quote: ibid, p. 51.
Page 17, callout quote: ibid, p. 54.
Page 19, callout quote: Kristin Johnson. *Unfortunate Emigrants: Narratives of the Donner Party.* Logan, Utah:
        Utah State University Press, 1996, p. 146.
Page 20, Line 14: Patrick Breen and Frederick J. Teggart, ed. *Diary of Patrick Breen, One of the Donner Party.*
        Berkeley, Calif.: University of California, 1910. p. 6.
Page 23, callout quote: ibid, p. 11.
Page 25, callout quote: Dale Morgan, ed. *Overland in 1846: Diaries and Letters of the California-Oregon Trail, Vol. 2.*
        Georgetown, Calif., Talisman Press, 1963. p. 328.

Printed in Canada.
052015   008825FRF15

TABLE OF CONTENTS

—— ◆ ——

CHAPTER 1

THE JOURNEY BEGINS

Strong oxen teams pulled nine covered wagons away from Springfield, Illinois, on April 14, 1846. The Donner and Reed families looked back as their familiar town slipped out of sight. They were headed west to California in search of a better life.

Wagon wheels wore deep grooves into the trails leading west across the American frontier. In 1846 about 2,700 **emigrants** set out like the Donner and Reed families. Many were ready to move away from the crowded cities in the East and Midwest. The West promised the chance for richer lives, better jobs, and the opportunity to claim available land. These pioneers imagined California as a sunny garden filled with fresh fruits and vegetables—a place where anything was possible.

"My father with tears in his eyes tried to smile as one friend after another grasped his hand in a last farewell. Mama was overcome with grief. At last the drivers cracked their whips, the oxen moved slowly forward and the long journey had begun."

—Virginia Reed Murphy, from her memoir *Across the Plains in the Donner Party*

Thousands of emigrants crossed the frontier to move out west in the mid-1800s.

Full of Hope

James Reed was a businessman from Illinois. He was wealthy enough to build a large, fancy wagon so that his family could travel out west comfortably. Even so, he dreamed of even greater riches and a better life in California.

George Donner was already a successful farmer in Illinois, but he was eager to settle in the rich farmland of California. He and his wife Tamsen, his brother Jacob, and his wife Elizabeth, were moving their 12 children out west. The children ranged in age from 3 to 14.

James and Margret Reed

Emigrants stocked up on food and supplies in Independence, Missouri, before the long journey west.

These pioneers were much like others who had gone before them. However, they would not stay on the well-traveled Oregon and California Trails. Instead, they would take a shortcut that was mentioned in a book called *The Emigrants' Guide to Oregon and California.* The author, Lansford Hastings, claimed that it would shorten the route by 300–400 miles (483–644 kilometers).

But Hastings published his book before he'd even traveled the shortcut himself. The book recommended crossing over steep mountains and across a wide desert. Travelers on horseback might be able to do it. But could slow-moving oxen pulling wide, heavy wagons make the journey?

Hastings was eager to help emigrants follow his new shortcut. In the spring of 1846, he and several other men set out on horseback from Sutter's Fort in present-day Sacramento, California. They trotted east as the Donners and Reeds rolled west.

A Smooth Beginning

In mid-May the Donners and Reeds arrived in Independence, Missouri, where the Oregon Trail began. Hundreds of travelers swarmed local shops purchasing supplies for the long journey west.

The Donners and Reeds and their nine wagons were part of the many heading west on the Oregon Trail. Ahead of them, they had more than 1,000 miles (1,609 km) of travel across mountains and rivers before they even reached Hastings' shortcut.

All travelers hurried along the trail in a race against winter. They needed to cross the high **Sierra Nevada Mountains** before snow blocked the trail, making travel nearly impossible. Getting trapped in the mountains during the frigid and stormy winter months could be deadly.

Hundreds of pioneers safely reached Oregon and California in 1846. But Hastings' shortcut would lead the group known today as the Donner Party to disaster.

CHAPTER

2

FOLLOWING
THE TRAIL

The travelers quickly got used to the slow, steady pace of the oxen as the wagon wheels creaked forward. But the trail did not always cooperate and traveling it could be challenging. River crossings were always dangerous because pioneers could lose their animals, supplies—or their lives. Crossing the gushing Big Blue River in Kansas proved particularly difficult as it was swollen from heavy rains.

The men cut down trees and built rafts to ferry their wagons across the water. After five days at the Big Blue River, the group quickly moved on. In a race against winter, there was no time to spare.

> "Indeed if I do not experience something far worse than I have yet done, I shall say the trouble is all in getting started ... I never could have believed we could have traveled so far with so little difficulty."
>
> —Tamsen Donner in a letter to a friend, June 16, 1846

An Easier River

As the **wagon trains** rolled through present-day Nebraska, they came to the muddy Platte River. The trail ran along the banks of the Platte for more than 450 miles (724 km). The wagons coasted along the flat land, traveling up to 20 miles (32 km) a day. Oxen feasted on the fresh grass along the riverbanks. Tamsen Donner wrote that their "journey so far has been pleasant." She went on to say that food was "plentiful," meat was "abundant," and drinking water was easy to find.

Warnings Ignored

In late June the group camped at Fort Laramie in southeastern Wyoming. They rested, took baths, and did laundry in the river. They also repaired their wagons and stocked up on food and supplies.

While there, Reed encountered an old army buddy. James Clyman had just taken Hastings' shortcut. He warned Reed that the shortcut was not suitable for bulky wagons. He advised Reed to stick to the traditional route. But Reed's group was already a week behind schedule, so Reed urged them to take the shortcut.

The trail beyond Fort Laramie climbed up along the jagged ridges of the Rocky Mountains. Most travelers walked alongside the wagons, while the oxen struggled with their heavy loads on the bumpy trail.

In mid-July a horseman approached them on the trail. He gave them a letter from Hastings, who said he would meet them at Fort Bridger in southwestern Wyoming. From there, he promised to guide them through the shortcut.

But when the Donners and Reeds arrived at Fort Bridger in late July, they were disappointed. Hastings had already left to lead another group of pioneers through the shortcut. However, he did leave a note instructing them to follow.

✑ FACT ✑

Edwin Bryant had started out in the same wagon train as the Donners and Reeds. But he arrived at Fort Bridger more than a week before the others. After discussing the Hastings Cutoff with a mountain man, Bryant wrote a letter to James Reed warning that the shortcut was not suitable for wagons. He left the letter with the fort's owners, but they never gave it to Reed. Instead, they encouraged Reed to take the Hastings Cutoff.

The Trail Splits

Shortly before Fort Bridger, the trail split. At the spot known as the "Parting of the Ways," the pioneers had to make a decision. Most turned northwest toward Fort Hall to continue on the Oregon Trail. But the Donners, Reeds, and other settlers who wanted to take Hastings' shortcut formed a new party. This new group, which included 74 people in 20 wagons, elected George Donner as their leader.

At Fort Bridger, the Donner Party had one last chance to return to the traditional route. But when they left Fort Bridger on July 31, they headed southwest.

THE OREGON AND CALIFORNIA TRAILS

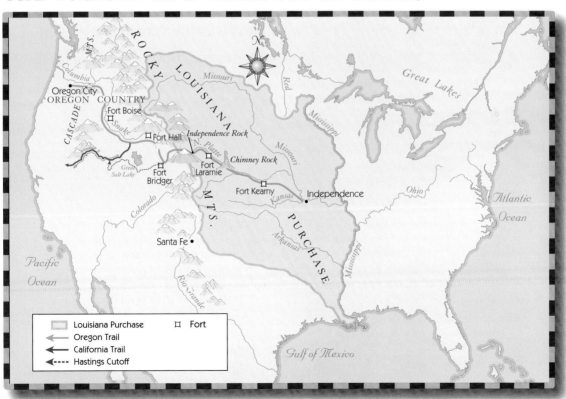

Legend:
- Louisiana Purchase
- Oregon Trail
- California Trail
- Hastings Cutoff
- Fort

CHAPTER 3
TROUBLE
ON THE TRAIL

The Donner Party followed wagon-wheel marks left by Hastings' group. The oxen trudged along the bumpy path, traveling about 10 miles (16 km) a day. Members of the party were confident they could reach Sutter's Fort in northern California in just seven weeks.

But after about a week traveling Hastings' shortcut, their pace slowed as they went deeper into the rugged Wasatch Mountains in present-day Utah.

Settlers struggled to move their bulky wagons along the ragged and bumpy trail through the mountains.

On August 6, they found another note from Hastings. He warned that the path ahead was too dangerous for wagons.

Reed and two men rode ahead to find Hastings. They found him a few days later, but he refused to return with them to help guide the Donner Party. Instead he told Reed about another route through the Wasatch Mountains. Once again, Hastings had never taken this path.

Reed traveled back to the Donner Party, blazing a path along an old Indian trail. He convinced the others to turn off the path they were traveling and head in a new direction. But they had to cut down trees and bushes just to clear a path. With oxen dragging wagons up steep slopes and through deep canyons, the group advanced just 2 miles (3.2 km) a day.

During this time 13 more people joined the Donner Party, bringing the total to 87. Toward the end of August, the worn-out emigrants escaped the Wasatch Mountains. But it had been nearly a month since they left Fort Bridger instead of the week Hastings had promised. It was now almost fall and they were still 600 miles (966 km) from California. The weary travelers found the tracks of Hastings' group—and another note.

"It was too late to turn back, for we were already far behind schedule and every day now brought the threat of getting snowbound in the Sierra Nevada Mountains."

—Virginia Reed Murphy, from her memoir *Across the Plains in the Donner Party*

Taking on the Desert

In the note Hastings warned of a desert ahead that would take two days to cross. The pioneers loaded their wagons with drinking water and grass for the oxen. On August 30, the drivers cracked their whips and started across the glittering white plains of Utah's Great Salt Lake Desert.

It took nearly a week to cross the 80-mile (129-km) desert. On the third day, the Donner Party's water supply ran out. Then about half the group's oxen ran away. As a result, the group lost a valuable source of transportation and food.

Wagon wheels got stuck in the soft sand and salt. Many settlers had to abandon their belongings and wagons, including the Reeds' fancy wagon. Tortured by thirst, they walked across the desert, carrying their belongings and small children.

☙ FACT ❧

Due to the difficult terrain it crossed, Hastings' route was not actually a shortcut. The Donner Party was led to believe that it would shorten the four- to five-month journey by two weeks. But if they had stuck to the traditional route, their journey would have been about a month shorter.

Utah's Great Salt Lake Desert averages less than 8 inches (20 centimeters) of rainfall per year. When the Donner Party ran out of water after just a couple of days, they had no way to get more.

By this time, the Donner Party was starting to feel hopeless. They also feared running out of food before reaching California. Charles Stanton and William McCutchen left the party to travel ahead to Sutter's Fort to bring back food.

Members of the Donner Party were relieved when they arrived at the Humboldt River on September 26. There the shortcut met up with the main trail to California. But winter was fast approaching. Because of the hard travel through the mountains and desert, the Donner Party was now far behind all the other wagons headed to California.

> "[T]he company decided to send Papa into the wilderness to die of slow starvation or to be murdered by the Indians ... My father was sent out into an unknown country without food or arms."
>
> —Virginia Reed Murphy, from her memoir
> *Across the Plains in the Donner Party*

Tempers Flare

After all the hardships they'd faced, the party members were cranky. Tempers flared on October 5 when wagon driver John Snyder and James Reed got into an argument. According to some witnesses, Snyder allegedly struck Reed in the head with his whip several times. When Margret Reed stepped in to stop Snyder from striking her husband, she too was hit with the whip. To defend himself and his wife, Reed pulled out his hunting knife and killed Snyder.

Horrified, the others demanded that Reed leave the group. He refused, but his wife convinced him to go. She urged him to ride ahead to Sutter's Fort and bring food back to them. In early October Reed left the party and headed west on horseback.

The emigrants also lost several animals when American Indians shot and killed 21 oxen with poisoned arrows. But the Donner Party pressed on.

The Homestretch

On October 16, the Donner Party arrived at the Truckee River, which flows through the Sierra Nevada Mountains from California. The swift-flowing river would guide the pioneers to within 100 miles (161 km) of their final **destination**. They eagerly followed the river to the base of the towering, granite peaks.

Artist Albert Bierstadt traveled to the American West in 1859 and 1863. The landscapes he witnessed there inspired many of his paintings, including this one titled *Among the Sierra Nevada Mountains*.

The Donner Party's hopes soared when they saw a familiar face on the mountain trail. More than a month after leaving with William McCutchen to get supplies, Charles Stanton was heading toward them with several mules loaded with food. He passed on the good news that the mountain paths were not usually blocked by snow until November. The travelers' hopes lifted.

"Hungry as we were, Stanton brought us something better than food—news. He had seen Papa ... not far from Sutter's Fort. Papa had been three days without food ... but he was still alive!"

—Virginia Reed Murphy, from her memoir *Across the Plains in the Donner Party*

Even so, the cold and cloudy weather made the settlers nervous, so they lumbered up the steep mountain trail. On October 31, they arrived just below a mountaintop. They left their wagons behind and tried to make it across the mountain's **summit**. But with the snow already waist-deep, it was nearly impossible. They decided to rest and try again the next day.

But their attempts the following day also failed. Then it snowed heavily overnight. The party awoke to find several feet of fresh snow burying the trail.

After traveling more than 2,000 miles (3,219 km), the Donner Party was only about 100 miles (161 km) from Sutter's Fort. But now 81 men, women, and children were trapped. They would have to spend the winter in the frigid Sierra Nevada Mountains.

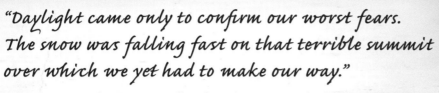

"Daylight came only to confirm our worst fears. The snow was falling fast on that terrible summit over which we yet had to make our way."

—John Breen, recalling his time as a member of the Donner Party

CHAPTER 4

TRAPPED IN THE MOUNTAINS

A few miles away from the rest of the party, the Donner family was trapped with a few others at Alder Creek. They had been held up because of a broken wagon **axle**. While trying to fix it, George Donner cut his hand badly. Nearly two dozen people crowded into shelters made with whatever they could find—logs, blankets, and brush covered with quilts and buffalo hides.

Meanwhile, the emigrants near the mountaintop grimly led their oxen back down to nearby Truckee Lake. There they found a cabin and built two more. Fifty-nine people huddled inside and waited for the snow to melt.

Days—then weeks—slowly passed as the snow continued to pile up. On November 30 at the Truckee Lake camp, Patrick Breen wrote in his journal that "no liv[e]ing thing without wings can get about."

Once the Donner Party members realized they couldn't get across the mountain in the deep snow, they went back down to Truckee Lake and set up camp.

On the other side of the mountains, James Reed was desperately trying to rescue them. On October 28 he had arrived at Sutter's Fort, where he gathered supplies and then headed back to the mountains. But he could not get past the chest-deep snowdrifts to reach those stranded in the mountains—including his wife and children.

Reed returned to California hoping to organize a large rescue party. But he had trouble finding tough, strong men because they were away fighting in the Mexican War (1846–1848). Reed briefly joined the war effort hoping to convince fellow soldiers to join his rescue party.

With the Truckee Lake camp buried in snow, a group of people headed off in search of help.

Misery and Hope

Meanwhile, hunger became the Donner Party's greatest enemy. After they had eaten all their food, they tried to hunt in the deep snow. But during winter there were few animals so high up in the mountains. Finally, they had to kill their starving cattle and oxen for food. They even dried the tough skin, or hide, to chew or to boil into a gluelike soup.

When the ox hides began to run out, the people became so desperate that they cooked mice that scrambled through their shelters. They even ate their pet dogs. In mid-December Baylis Williams was the first to die at the Truckee Lake camp.

Group members knew they would all starve to death if they waited for the spring. So on December 16 a group of 17 men and women left the Truckee Lake camp in search of help. They were weak with hunger and afraid of leaving the camp. But they were hopeful that they could climb down the mountains and bring help to their families. This group became known as "Forlorn Hope."

Most of the Forlorn Hope members wore homemade snowshoes made of sticks and ox hides. Six days after the group left, their food supply ran out.

When a blizzard caught the Forlorn Hope members without shelter, four of them died. After several days without food, the survivors were too weak to continue on their mission. In order to survive, they ate the leather straps on their snowshoes and the flesh of their dead companions.

Patrick Breen began keeping a diary while the Donner Party was stranded in the mountains. This entry is from February 25, 1847.

"[P]rovisions scarce, hides are the only article we depend on, we have a little meat yet, may God send us help."

—Patrick Breen's journal entry, January 17, 1847

The Forlorn Hope party continued on for two more weeks. With their feet bleeding from frostbite, they finally stumbled into a Miwok village in mid-January 1847. The Indians fed them acorn bread and pine nuts.

Some members of the tribe helped guide William Eddy 18 miles (29 km) to Johnson's Ranch, a settlement in present-day Wheatland, California. A group of men from the settlement followed Eddy's bloody footprints back to the Miwok village. They guided the remaining survivors (one man and five women) back to Johnson's Ranch. The Forlorn Hope party had traveled nearly 90 miles (145 km). A messenger continued on to Sutter's Fort—40 miles (64 km) away—where news of the Donner Party's terrible situation quickly spread.

John Sutter contributed supplies and organized a rescue party to save survivors from the Donner Party.

A Difficult Rescue

In early February a rescue party organized by John Sutter left Johnson's Ranch for the dangerous trek over the mountains. They trudged knee-deep into the snow carrying 50-pound (23-kilogram) packs of food on their backs. As they neared Truckee Lake, they estimated that the snow was 30 feet (9 meters) deep.

Finally on February 18 they arrived at the camp near Truckee Lake. They watched in horror as men, women, and children crawled out of snow-covered shelters. They were skin and bones. At the Alder Creek camp, the rescuers found the Donner family in even worse condition. Since the emigrants had become snowbound, 13 people had died at the Truckee Lake and Alder Creek camps. To survive, many at the camps were also forced to eat the flesh of the dead.

"We looked all around but no living thing ... was in sight and we thought that all must have perished. We raised a loud halloo and then we saw a woman emerge from a hole in the snow. As we approached her several others [came] out of the snow. They were gaunt with famine and I never can forget the horrible, ghastly sight they presented."

—George Tucker, a 16-year-old member of the first Donner Party rescue team

CHAPTER 5

CALIFORNIA AT LAST

John Sutter had put Reason Tucker and Aquilla Glover in charge of leading the first group to safety. This first group consisted of seven rescuers and 23 survivors, mostly children ranging in age from 3 to 14. Shortly after they started out, Patty Reed, age 8, and Thomas Reed, age 4, were sent back to camp because they were too weak to travel. Three others died on the way.

Unaware that Sutter had already sent a search party, James Reed had gone to what is now San Francisco to raise money for his own rescue group. Reed's group headed for the Sierra Nevada in late February. They crossed paths with Tucker's group on February 26. The next day, Reed shared a brief but joyful reunion with his wife and two of his children. He was astonished to find out that his entire family was still alive.

The Donner family was less fortunate than the Reeds. They lost more members than any other family. Jacob Donner, his wife Elizabeth, and two of their sons died at the Alder Creek camp. Two other sons died on the way to California with the rescue teams. Only three of their children reached California alive.

Tamsen Donner refused to leave her dying husband, George, to join a rescue party. They both died before the last rescue team arrived. But their five daughters all survived the journey to California.

It took three months and four rescue parties to bring all of the survivors of the Donner Party to California. The last survivor, Louis Keseberg, reached Sutter's Fort on April 29, 1847.

Louis Keseberg

FACT

All five of George and Tamsen Donner's daughters survived the terrible ordeal in the mountains and made it safely to California. But they were also orphans. An older couple who lived near Sutter's Fort raised Georgia, Eliza, and Leanna. Their sister Frances and their cousin Mary were taken in by James and Margret Reed.

Moving On

Of the 81 members of the Donner Party who were trapped in the mountains, 36 died. The 45 survivors finally made it to California, where they moved into new homes and started over. They found jobs and started businesses.

All across America newspapers spread the story of the Donner Party. Their journey was full of mistakes and suffering. But it was also full of courage and determination. The Donner Party served as a lesson for the thousands of travelers who followed, seeking riches in the West. Not even their tragic tale could stop settlers from moving west, especially after gold was discovered near Sutter's Fort in 1848. Between 1849 and 1854, more than 140,000 pioneers moved out west on the Oregon and California Trails.

TIMELINE

April 14, 1846
The Donner and Reed families leave Springfield, Illinois, and begin their journey to California.

July 19, 1846
The Donner Party officially forms when a new group splits off from the main group. The Donner Party heads toward the Hastings Cutoff, a proposed shortcut.

1846

May 29, 1846
Sarah Keyes, Margret Reed's mother, dies. She is buried along the trail in northeastern Kansas.

October 5, 1846
James Reed kills John Snyder during an argument near the Humboldt River. Reed is asked to leave the group, so he heads to Sutter's Fort to get food and supplies for his family.

MORE WOMEN SURVIVED THAN MEN

Twenty-eight of the males in the Donner Party died, compared to only eight females. Why did the women of the Donner Party survive the winter better than the men?

Some scientists believe the men wore themselves out more quickly with the hard work of building shelters and searching for food. Or perhaps, like George Donner, they were wounded while performing dangerous tasks.

Scientists also wonder if the women were able to stay warmer and healthier more easily. Their bodies are often smaller and generally have more heat-trapping body fat than those of men.

It is also possible that more women survived because of their families. They were busy helping their children, husbands, and friends stay alive. Of the 15 snowbound men who were traveling alone without families, only two survived.

December 16, 1846
The Forlorn Hope group leaves the Truckee Lake camp in search of help.

December 15, 1846
Baylis Williams is the first person to die at the Truckee Lake camp.

Mid-January 1847
The Forlorn Hope group stumbles upon a Miwok village. The Indians guide William Eddy to the town of Johnson's Ranch to get help.

Mid-April 1847
A fourth and final rescue group arrives at the Truckee Lake camp. Louis Keseberg, the sole survivor, is rescued.

1847

November 4, 1846
After an overnight blizzard leaves 10-foot (3-m) snowdrifts, the Donner Party realizes they are trapped in the mountains.

February 18, 1847
The first rescue party arrives at the Truckee Lake camp.

March 10, 1847
A third relief group heads to the Truckee Lake and Alder Creek camps. Tamsen Donner sends her daughters with the rescuers but refuses to leave her dying husband.

GLOSSARY

axle (AK-suhl)—a rod in the center of a wheel around which the wheel turns

destination (des-tuh-NAY-shuh)—the place to which one is traveling

emigrant (E-muh-grant)—a person who leaves one area to go live in another

gaunt (GAWNT)—very thin, usually because of illness or suffering

Sierra Nevada Mountains (see-AIR-uh nuh-VA-duh MOUN-tuhns)—a mountain range in California and Nevada that is about 400 miles (644 km) long and 70 miles (113 km) wide.

summit (SUHM-it)—the highest point of a mountain

wagon train (WAG-uhn TRANE)—a group of pioneers traveling together in covered wagons, often in a single-file line

READ MORE

Domnauer, Teresa. *Life in the West.* True Books: American History. New York: Children's Press, 2010.

Hester, Sallie. *Diary of Sallie Hester: A Covered Wagon Girl.* First-Person Histories. North Mankato, Minnesota: Capstone Press, 2014.

Kravitz, Danny. *Surviving the Journey: The Story of the Oregon Trail.* Adventures on the American Frontier. North Mankato, Minnesota: Capstone Press, 2015.

Sandler, Martin W. *Who Were the American Pioneers?: And Other Questions about Westward Expansion.* Good Question! New York: Sterling Children's Books, 2014.

INTERNET SITES

FactHound offers a safe, fun way to find Internet sites related to this book. All of the sites on FactHound have been researched by our staff.

Here's all you do:

Visit *www.facthound.com*

Type in this code: 9781491448984

Super-cool stuff! Check out projects, games and lots more at
www.capstonekids.com

CRITICAL THINKING USING THE COMMON CORE

1. Why was it so important that emigrants traveling the Oregon and California Trails start the journey in the springtime? (Key Ideas and Details)

2. Do you believe that Lansford Hastings was solely responsible for the Donner Party's suffering? Why or why not? Support your answer with details from the text. (Text Types and Purposes)

3. Take a look at the map on page 11, which compares the traditional route to California to the Hastings Cutoff. Do you think the Hastings Cutoff looks 300–400 miles shorter? Knowing the risks, would you have taken the shortcut if you were in the Donner Party? (Integration of Knowledge and Ideas)

INDEX